Black Ice & Fire

Poems 1974-2014

James Ross Kelly

Black Ice & Fire

Poems 1974-2014

by James Ross Kelly

...where breath comes from, where breath has its beginnings, where drama, has to come from, where, the coincidence is, all acts spring

Charles Olson —*Projective Verse*—1950.

Black Ice & Fire—Poems 1974-2014

Copyright 2021—James Ross Kelly

Poems have appeared in the following publications: *The Rogue Valley Weekly War Whoop & Moral Volcano*; Ashland, Oregon; *Poems for a Scorpio Moon & Others*, Stumbling Bear Press Ashland Oregon; *Westwind Review*, Ashland, Oregon; *Open Sky* Seattle; *Siskiyou Journal* Ashland, Oregon; *Don't Read This*, Ashland, Oregon; *Table Rock Sentinel*, Medford, Oregon; *Poetry Motel*, Duluth, Minnesota *Sliver Birch Press*, Los Angeles; *The Red Gate & Other Poems*; a hand-set letter press chapbook published by Cowan & Tetley; 1984, Vancouver, B.C.; *Ray's Road Review*, *Lucky Jefferson*, *Raw Art Review*, *Edify*, and *The Effects of Grace*.

Cover photo of Mountain Lady Slipper (*Cypripedium montanum*) by Author

Book Design by:

UnCollected Press
8320 Main Street, 2nd Floor
Ellicott City, MD 21043

For more books by UnCollected Press:
www.therawartreview.com

First Edition 2021
ISBN: 978-1-7360098-4-0

for Anita

Contents

Poem for the Beer Drunk Fishermen 1

Down a long road 2

My Grandfather's Farm 5

The Vet is coming at two 8

The Red Gate 10

If I look out the window 12

Where do you live? 13

Lady slipper 14

Then suddenly 15

Perhaps in Heaven 16

Having panted 17

In a Grove by the River 18

Favorite Meal 19

Coition 20

Six Pac, on Ice, & on Fire 21

Guns 27

We awoke once 28

Bill Smith 29

An Unkindness of Ravens 30

Since January 32

Cheeseburger 33

All That Is Natural 34

I will continue to seek visions & 36

Pacific Yew 37

Two Eleven-Year-Old Girls 40

These Pelicans	42
The House Was on The Corner	44
Anger of a Kind	47
Death & Poetry	49
Integral	50
Canticle for Duke	51
This Abundant Life	53
Del Santee's Irish Uncle	55
The Forester	57
I saw Ted Barr Smiling	59
After Last Call	61
Voyager has now left the solar system	62
All That Is Natural	63
Independence Day	65
Demoiselle	66
I planted in the Trinity Alps	67
First of Three encounters with Lions	68
A Psalm	69
St. Somebody's	71
Fall of the Hipeoisie (Hip-WA-ZEE)	72
Venus Void of course	74
Why the Cold War was Cold	78
Brief description of Creation	79
Mall Santa	80
Starting just before 1970	82
Without God	84
Tramp Harbor	85

The Green Flash	87
We are not human	88
The Chink-oh-pin	90
My Car	91
Two voices from a campfire	92
Hard Believing	93
Wolves & Working Men	94
Sunflower heads	103
Love is like	104
First Contact	105
At the Counsel of Oak Flat	106
Bear kill on deer hunt	107
Living the Dream	109

Poem for the Beer Drunk Fishermen
Who were Lost at Sea
Off the Crescent City Pier
In the tidal wave of 1964—

fools on a spree
six-packs underarms
waving at deodorized
fumes of unreason
before the surf was up
lost long before they
were found between sausages
hamburgers and the
necessity of a mortgage
to come home to
filleted and floundered
between fishing boats
and the fuel of the barge
flipping end over end on
what was to be
the flotsam and jetsam
of what cannot live
in the terrible sound of
creation and beauty
in cataclysmic mandate
as water arcing over league
upon league roll over roll
fathom upon depth naming
an unforgiving– *"You!"*
at the beer tipping
realization of the mistake
about the smallness of what
was thought to ought to be

Down a long road

Looking down
a long road where
there could be
a place we all belong
beginning each day again
our lives becoming alive
to each other & it is
where we go
on this way to be,
despite a rampant call of noise,
between laughter we could
be roses, or white, white
poppies amidst what we
call to be ourselves, alive
beautiful & blended
with time & sorrow
it should be that our
days are long spinning
turns toward life
& that flowered brightness of
& in only ourselves, togethered
& astonished with the day as a point of light
& time the unthought-of container amid
night's black rest with other points of light
      brilliant
      & waiting

Now these Present Ghosts

If you walked through the front door
with the thumb latch key &
Took a right you would walk into the living room
& continue on &
With a left turn before the bedroom
There were worn wooden stairs
& upstairs were rooms of equal size
Sparely furnished &
On a hanger in the east room
My father's uniform hung, festooned as
Staff Sergeant, Eisenhower jacket
& campaign ribbons on the front
Then a hall & door closed on the attic
That ran half the length of the upstairs,
& if you opened the attic
Door a window from the south kept it pretty hot
I would play in the attic when it was cool
I remember finding Indian head pennies under loose
Floorboards, other than books
I cannot remember any of the contents of
The attic, boxes, I suppose, it was not empty but the
Smell was clean & warm & the two rooms of
The upstairs seemed strange as no one ever slept there
Wooden dressers with no clothes & the east room
Was a scintillating white...
The years I lived in this house, haunt me now
As it did not then, the presentiment of what was to come
I suppose, these years left a hollow place
As I would be an orphan at nine, we lived by the
Slow running Walnut River,
& the east room's white walls
Are now these present ghosts from when that house
Bore relevant-to-me lives, & heard my
Grandmother sing arias,

With radio opera, or an old cowboy song
& I remember
The smell my father's boots
As I longed for
His coming home hour,
When work boots,
& clothes came off on the back porch,
& after a bath & dinner, & I remember,
The open door of his returning good humor.

My Grandfather's Farm

He did not homestead
As his grandfather had,
During Bloody Kansas, but
He was born in a sod house,
& his father, an immigrant at nine
Learned carpentry &
Built a wooden house on another farm
Around 1884 & he, a second generation
Norwegian, with an English mother
Who had insisted on Anglicizing
The name Nygaard, to Thompson
He, the second son, took to Cowboy as soon as he could,
Worked for a Texas Ranger named Crump,
Went on one cattle drive from Texas to Abilene
& an expedition against small farmers, which were putting
Up barb wire & all this after as a lad,
He had seen prairie chickens
Fly up in such great numbers as to block out the sun
& he had seen the Dalton Brother's
Rob a bank — a wilding with six
Guns drawn & a getaway, &
He had tried to fight in the
Spanish war but was sent
Back from Florida when
He was discovered too young, &
After returning, he was breaking
A horse & was thrown
& in the dust & picking himself up
He heard an old timer at the edge of the corral
Laugh, and yell, "Remember the Mane!"
That year he was thrown from a horse again,
& compound fractured his leg below the knee,

& he had crawled three miles
back to the ranch house
Where they put him in a buck board wagon
& drove him ten miles to a doctor,
& he showed me those scars, & I heard a conversation
He had with an old timer who lived up on the South fork
Of Little Butte Creek in a cabin here in Oregon,
& how in 1901
They, unbeknownst to each other,
Had both been at a rodeo
at the 101 Ranch in Oklahoma
& where he saw a young Will Rogers, & a
Federal guard had old Geronimo in a cage,
& let him out to make the fierce old man shoot a buffalo
Tied to a stake, & they & many of the cowboys thought
That a disgusting spectacle, but they ate of the Buffalo
Two years later, he courted my grandmother,
daughter of third generation
German American family from Ohio,
That had 500 acres of bottom land,
& sons either unwilling, or unable to farm, &
In September of 1903, my Grandfather was feeding hogs
for the old man from a wagon &
His father-in-law to be, was sitting on the fence
Twenty feet from him, when a lightning bolt
Struck the old man, & turned him to charcoal
& knocked my Grandfather out of the wagon
& he & Grandmother married in October
& pretty much the day of the lightning strike
they inherited their farm
& he was successful for almost thirty years,
most of his children living
& graduating from High School,
& stories of family life began to abide,

All I wish I could have recorded
The scores of farm hands he employed,
All thinking well of him as a fair man,
& neighbors & stock bought & sold,
& wheat crops & corn crops
& hogs, & cattle, & early machines of mechanized agriculture,
Like a corn chopper that took his middle finger,
& the time he threw the Klan off his property
When they tried to recruit him,
& neighbors, & the time the tornado took off the barn door,
When he was trying to get the horses out,
& then it fell on him
& broke his back, laying him up for a time
In the hospital, & then Depression came &
He & my Grandmother & my mother,
Their youngest, had to drive
Away in a buckboard wagon, pulled by a team of horses
From their property and prosperity, this lightening
Came in the form of a squall of bloody Kansas bankers,
After wheat & hogs, & corn crops
That mortgaged the farm became worthless,
While down in Texas, Lyndon Johnson changed all that, &
Saved Texas farmers from far off Washington
& knowing this, years later,
My Grandfather was happy to vote for LBJ,
While the rest of my family,
Who though they revered the oil painting
Of the stone farmhouse they had grown up in,
Voted Goldwater, complaining that
The government was too large.

The Vet is coming at two

My Dog is dying
Under the crepe myrtle
In full blossom & drifting
Down over him & me &
My wife & the Vet is coming
At two, he is 14 & had the full
Dog experience, me rescuing him from
A rancher who got him as a stray
Into his ranch & announced he
Had too many dogs, & his wife
Knowing he would shoot him &
I worked with her & she asked 12 years ago,
"Would you like a nice dog?"
& I saw him and said, "Hi buddy,"
& he sat down right beside me & took
A pet & he's been my Buddy ever since
For me & my son & my wife, he has
Chased cows on my rancher buddy's 7,000-acre ranch,
With Cow-dog English Shepherds in Eastern Oregon,
& had three years of running with Walker Hounds
On Black bear chases in Alaska, with my hunting buddy
Biologist & once treed, we then took pictures
& petted up the dogs, we let all the bears go &
Once he treed a bear on his own,
But he would come back to the truck
If the Walker hounds had a five-mile chase
He in his Airedale/Rottweiler
compact 90 lb. frame defended our yard
From a marauding German shepherd,
& after the stitch up
I had him neutered, & he was still hard on cats but
He learned to live with the one we had,
Early on I saw that he would point cats

Paw up and tail straight like a bird dog &
Well, I have had to pay a number of vet bills
to stitch up felines
& just two weeks ago feeble as he is
One wandered into his backyard
& he tried for one last biting of the cat,
tipping over the lawn chairs,
Table & umbrella, & barbecue,
He always had the seeming happy dog smile
Even now that he cannot move his hind legs
& he quivers in pain
& the Vet is coming at two, & my dear wife
Has been weeping for three days &
The crepe myrtle blossoms are falling on him
& the Vet is coming at two.

The Red Gate

That last time I was to the farm
where running through creeks, chasing
small birds and my imagination, I
had grown up (in stature at least)
there was a red gate my Grandfather had built

Much of the paint had blistered and peeled
as its weight had pulled the corner post
forward toward the earth that it also
had leaned for, still functional but barely so

Fashioned with boards and bolt that
had gone through hand augured holes by
brace and bit—I still remember
that tools' shininess from years of use

The gate separated the farm from
the adjacent well-to do horse ranch
where fine Arabians pawed at the
sawdust in tight functional stalls

The west corner had a barn that had
burned several winters back
all the animals had gotten out
though, the gate was only five feed away it stood,
a bit charred but still latched to the fence

It had swung open mostly for bartered loads
of hay and occasionally for myself, to get closer
to a fox or deer in the next field and sometimes
to deliver Christmas cakes to affluent neighbors

The farm changed hands to distant relations
by marriage, who after a funeral came offering
condolences and money — I stood there looking
at its form as the content of memories, of ghosts
of the distance of wealth, of long-ago laughter
of the presence of sorrow, that screeched

like a rusty hinge

If I look out the window

blonde, sunglasses
dark suited miniskirt
large belt
w/tight beige pants
could be a model.
standing at an outside table
of this coffee house
if I look out the window
from drinking my joe
I cannot see anything else but her
talking through her cell phone device
clipped in her ear, just barely perceptible
adamant, using both hands
for expression, articulate
it seems, making points,
striding around, a little round table,
& between chairs
as if a stage
& this was performance, &
this is all normal now...
less than twenty years ago
this would have been observed
as psychotic behavior,
talking to someone who is
obviously not there & not holding a phone,
or, rehearsing a play
my friends, some of them
think the same of me
when I pray.

Where do you live?

We may be light
Moving monuments
Spiral informative testaments
Seemingly from void
Lifting emission of inception
Cloud illumining hopes,
Of skyshine,
Invisibly shining back
Light phosphoresce in dark
As subtle beacons,
Transceivers for life, &
Noise attempts to drown the transmission out,
Longing for love, the message
Sent long ago, but not in a bottle while we are
Still wading shores darkened by loss
Of knowing, we are sleeping shining
Bread eaters & we are, lost in fog
Hungering, hardly black or white, wondering
From the wondering machine
& color coming in the message from
The source ladder, a spiraled ladder
Transmitted from beyond & inside
& a voice says, "Come and see!"

Lady slipper

Lady
slipper
Lady's slipper
dew dropped orchid girl
at dawn...

"a fool for her stockings,"
someone said I was for hers,
& I admit there were times
sharp high heeled
imprints walked
over the backbone
of my soul,
because I let them

    & I let them

Lady slipper
Lady's slipper
dew dropped orchid girl
at dawn...
long gone

Then suddenly

At dusk,
The Vaux's swifts that had been up
& down the river feeding on flying insects,
Began to draw close & come together
With high, rapid twittering,
High whistled chipping,
In ever tightening circles,
Swirling & swirling,
They all go up to spin together,
In a great pinwheel-like circle,
Coming more & more altogether
Directly above the chimney,
Then suddenly,
As one morphic resonant being,
They come down,
& into a whirling black-funnel-down
Tornado-like cloud gyre,
Fifty feet in height, above the house
& then into-the-chimney
In a second or two,
Full of this day's hatch settling & chittering for
Brick gripped sleep.

Perhaps in Heaven

Perhaps in Heaven
Since we really do not have information
To concisely presume otherwise,
The universe as
We know it, is contained
In a large room where doors
Open and close, & exactly
As Jacob observed, Angels
Are busily rising or
Descending to earth & perhaps other galaxies,
& that this, quite contrary to any cynical view,
Is the one of the most important of rooms...
& our entry and exit—all of us..

    Is well known.

Having panted

Having panted
In the early summer heat
A quarter mile away,
A doe drinks
From a heated
Brackened pool
Small rolling
Just dislodged
Rocks from a dry
Hillside, brings
Long eared attention
To break in hot silence,
Warm drops break circles
On the surface from a
Black nose poised
To listen & then
Drink again

In a Grove by the River

In a grove by the river
Landlord walks, counting
First fruits six months out &

Summons pruners to these rows, &
Directs water from this
River to supplement the rain
Oversees the cutting, helps
Stack limbs & fires off
Bonfires while
Mist moistens up the air &
Smoke drifts past willows
At the water's edge
Blue heron flies
Out from an eddy as the tractor
Loudly makes its turn

Now fruit will grow
Larger when harvest
Finally comes

Landlord walks on
Riverbank & surveys what
He has done.

Favorite Meal

On entering the Tehama County library
I find a sumptuous oak table then
Locate the latest National Geographic
& learn the favorite meal
Of the Inuit,
In Isortoq, Greenland
Is seal,
Dipped in ketchup & mayonnaise

Coition

was after
dried roses
that ether-death
sickness of after
smell gone
that last warm cold goodness of after
longtime
meant promise of after
cigarette/heavy
breathing of
after
toilet flush
after
padding feet back to
a rustle of covers
of after, after
slamming doors behind
strained voices of
after beginning before
an end of after always
before the bright
deaf rendering thunder
silent dark flashing
shudder of after
& together before
a memory
empty & alone

Six Pac, on Ice, & on Fire

      -I-

I would have brought a flower,
but roses will not bloom save in
fetid hothouses with this
spring rain now colder for
a higher elevations snow
I would have brought a flower,
but quince somehow will not do,
and the daffodils are so very
elegantly too plain; there are
no wild lilacs yet and the lily
has naturally one more month
      underground

I would have brought you a flower
from some other planet; where enchanted
by its own light and fragrant from
the stem expectations become light
winds and old memories reside
      on a special moon

I would have brought you a flower
but it may be that each severed
stem may cause pain on a star somewhere
and it is in the spring that women
are the petals of a long winter's hope
bringing longitudes from history
for at least the clouds and something
      surer than romance

-II-

Like a just
cracked chrysalis
an open door
before drying begins,
flight as an interim
remains with the now
dried shell of love
we had & what could

begin again is that
long time between
old age & the Andes
      flying, flying,
            flying

I could wait for
the South Pole
to melt into the North
& it still would not
be as long as a week
w/out your love
or a day thinking it
may never come again

-III-

Past now the fall's brown & ochre
leaves a round smell
& must of after rain,
like after love, as
union & meeting of flank
& loin like the various
conceptions future a ride
with winter's underground

decay streaked mycelial
urge & subterranean closure
of where we are & this
our own life as expression
& objective, like the dank
smell behind every fragrant
rose & estrangement behind

every kiss & embrace/trick is,
that beauty in and of herself
belies the moleish worm worn
propensity of decay to show now
life as petal freshflower breath

meetings of a moment in the deep,
deep—deep pools
of our own eyes

-IV-

Broad based blue mountains
maintain an outer edge whose
forests slope down as curve
on hip to smooth a desert or
the watery trap of this valley,
with river & creeks, given
enclosures for low breasted
foothills in related contours
that blend the white oak with
chaparral, the fox grass green
with spring & then short brown
with summers dryness hidden
in the ripe sticky loam of
falls coming winter where we are

    a folding of you I touch,
    a caress of inner thigh
    the hardness of your
    tongued nipple rising as
    hips move toward each other,
    & then this inner entry of
    touch & kiss with pelvic
    push & pull holding & giving
    to let go together in an
    ambient headlong rush of love
    & passion or both or neither
    a void of self, togethered alone

the deep big bellied
Pacific Ocean calls
after Australia & the
Philippines while up
on Tinian where Hiroshima's
death was launched a Peace
committee & good intentions

planted a garden
dedicated to what may not
happen again; to date nothing
yet grows there, while palm
fronds sway before the wind
in creaking leeward arcs of
sentient change, a year is a day
a month is a year & can ever the hardness
of our hearts
melt without fear?

-V-

I could be still or move
with this earth & its need
of regular revolution
tipping in axial propensity
toward, not circles,
        but elliptical
irregularity which is
regular & calculable

perigee/apogee,
the farthest and closest
revolving moment
you connect me somehow
to movement & revolution
a still resurrection
of love & knowing

-XI-

Hope was off the top of my head
    Where the blooming
Pear trees go & lately
    Replicating fir & tamarack
Lined ridges
    Whose recent snow
Reminds us below
    That spring has its elevations
As well as latitudes.

The sun's rays bring fast light
    passing clouds over the valley bound
& the slow pervasive glow in foothills &
    mist enshrouded ravines.

Crop duster does a wing over
    & picks up another
Blossom lined orchard
    As four ravens fly over this road
While a 727 disappears with a roar into white

    Down here though, near the airport
An entire blooming orchard across from
    the posh *Mon Desir* restaurant
Gives way for tract homes
    bull dozed in mid bloom these
    Pear trees tipped over like
    murdered ballerinas in white tutus,
    their upturned rooted toe shoes in the air

Guns

Sporadic gunfire
in the distance
of the hills,
& the Fall's hunt
was always
the Octobered drysmell
of chaparral
& that clean mean click
of manzanita breaking
through the drivers,
coming down & out of
far recessed ravines,
where the large
lone blacktail bucks waited,
their solitude
for the coming rut,
only to be flushed
out of almost impassable
hiding, & then the high
powered velocity of the crack
of a modern firearm
delivers the yearly venison,
tabled later
in the fall,
perennially seasoned
w/salt & black peppered
for biscuits & gravy,
the crisp taste of the High Cascade,
I remember how
our bitch border collie shepherd dog
would cower in her corner,
teeth chattering, uncontrollably, and shaking,
shaking, at that near & far rifle fire.

We awoke once

We awoke once
Having slept under the stars &
On a red dawn solstice
Lavender light
& walked naked
to edge of your
roof garden
as sun's rays became
another's midnight
& in a whirl
I saw us descendants
of a beginning incessant motion,
inhabitants on a small sphere
whose turning
lends music
from universe & spring
a little off key &
on the docket
recipients of circles
set in motion, then
figments to one another, now
figures to our heirs &
I did not know how
to tell you
before you left for India that
I thought pantheism
was a clever lie.

Bill Smith

When
I was in the Army
I came across one
Bill Smith,
Who had lived
On Main Street
In Pleasantville, New Jersey
& was no ordinary man,
Other than that,
There was nothing
Remarkable about him.

An Unkindness of Ravens

On the death of poet David Lloyd Whited

It had been over four fortnights since my friend
David died, his widow at his deathbed calling
Me & asking me to speak to him
Through the phone, he in a coma
Children and Marian around so, I panicked &
I prayed the only Christian prayer
I could think of, "Lord bring him back
We need him here, his good cheer and we
Need more of him and Lord don't take him!"
I'll apologize to no man for my panic

When his wife arrived from her
Work that Friday he first allowed that he'd not gone,
To work as he was feeling bad, & minutes later he
Was on the floor, that Friday night
Having collapsed trying to sit up with Marian's help
On his couch, didn't feel good that day,
& he stiffened up and went to the floor
I was 700 miles down I-5, I could not go
& there was no good outcome surmised by doctors
The Poet's heart had given way

In Alaska I saw repeatedly every deer season
An Unkindness of Ravens as they are called
When in a feeding frenzied group to
Herald every after kill of blacktail deer,
A snow laden clamor of raven and eagle
Blood on white snow unsympathetic
As most obituaries but louder, & yet
I know only
the antidote of fond memory

David & I as young men
Drank and read our poems aloud
& reading poems, we crawled through bars & bistros,
& fished behind the Snake River dams
& off the derelict sand barge on Maurey Island
& caught ling and true Cod & sharks out of the
Puget Sound
I carried him out of at least three bars & one night
Off the Tramp Harbor pier
This was the man that wrote:
"Sadness Drives a Fast Red Car"

He died Sunday morning after Thanksgiving
I did not go to the funeral, did not know of a wake
Cremated out of the hospital & as there is usually
These days, no acknowledgement of the body as a rite
A memorial in a church in Tacoma was due
Work friends, one brother, grieving
Marian & son & daughters
I called her the morning of the funeral
& I asked her to open all the windows
In their little house on the Puget Sound
At the mouth of Judd Creek
When she left to go to Tacoma.

My good friend David is dead

Since January

Waiting for
Japanese bottle brush
To bloom
Having counted on whiteness of
These now, fading camellia
Since January have bloomed my
East wall & the roses
Have gone to sea blooming like
Frigates w/all their Joseph's coat colors hoisted
In the backyard & on the west side long stem reds,
Are rowing splendor for my Queen Wife's delight,
& Cana Lilly's are taking up arms
In the shady eastside, & back yard
w/grapevine climbing & opposite a flowering plum
Having flowered & next to a sleepy quaking
Aspen wakes with every slight breeze, now
There's Bougainvillea on the front deck
& this morning
Brinkman's Black birds are over my head
like little jet airplanes,
An acorn woodpecker hammers in the oaks,
Brandt's winging fast following river
Upstream, & cormorants going down,
passing a Great Blue heron
Who, flying like a long-legged-guitar picker
is going back the other way,
& past my chair, as I am sitting there,
sipping cheap good French roast
At seven am & no, this is not license—a bald eagle
Swoops down, after a fish in the Sacramento,
& a slight breeze sends petunia smell
& now, domesticatedly wild about abundant life, I
Absolutely had to write this poem

Cheeseburger

she ordered a cheeseburger
on a French roll with only a
half order of French fries for
she says, a full one was much
too much, now she cleans her glasses
& sips a small coke/all this
before she had removed
two sweaters &
first one comes over her head as
her back arches and breasts arch
almost skywards & the second

likewise, overhead & now
down to yellow t-shirt
where both these actions
caught three
males @ this lunch counter, caused
one poem/& maybe
has something to do with a breeze
laden palm tree somewhere in
the Society Islands, I stay for
my bacon cheeseburger, & it is rare.

All That Is Natural

Holding love
at arm's length
as hype gets
in the way
more, thought to be
better, rather
than there being
no such thing
as better but
only good
& part of what is...

Around the corner it is the same
evident individual difference
of selfishness
proffered like multi-verse
of which there is no
evidence, when before
another is...
defined as breath
& even unindigenous
& maligned as they are,
starlings can fly in unison,
yet, they cranky nest & breed & feed
in small groups, then move off in
great black mobial swirl perceptive
but not perceiving, an unseen morphic field
of each other proffering
them as one, moving
north or south on the continent
thought of as nuisance birds & could it be
that this other perceived nuisance of
all that is natural will

Perhaps one resurrected day, come home
to roost when we see information that
binds it all, with which we perceive
this perception—beyond any physical realm
becoming Supernatural

I will continue to seek visions & count on my friends to know everything

I dreamed I was in 1962,
in a department store
dressing room w/ Lana Turner,
or someone who said she was, Lana Turner,
& who told me she had to adjust
her nylon stocking & did not mind
if I looked—and I awoke and remembered that year
I had been in a desk behind the cloak room in my
eighth grade English teacher's classroom
who hated me, and whose name I have long ago forgotten
I had been put there for being a smart ass
& was napping & Joanie & Janet, whom I had known
since they were girls, came back there,
but that year they were no longer girls,
& really did adjust their stockings
& they really did let me watch,
skirts hiked up & looking athletic
& as they pulled on the
black back seamed nylons on their legs
while hitching up garter belts, &
I knew at that moment,
there was something I had,
that would not go away

Pacific Yew

I was once paid
to survey Yew trees
in Old Growth forests
in Oregon near Crater Lake, where
mammoth Douglas fir & White fir
covered the landscape, rolling sides
of mountains, the Yew were generally
in wet areas, crevices of creeks,
they grew as attendant soldiers to the large conifers
the Yew only fifty to sixty feet tall,
the oldest of them
lining the feeder streams that stretched downward
to Creeks that all ran to the Rogue River
the surrounding clearcuts were littered with their
brothers & sisters as they are sexed male & female
loggers put them into large piles
to be burned as unmerchantable

In Canada they made them into beautiful
hardwood flooring, & after closing a bar in
British Columbia I was drinking beer
at a timber fallers home & complemented
him on his floor as it was gorgeous red hues
& blond running throughout the lengths of the boards,
& I asked him what kind of wood
it was, as I had installed wood floors
for about as brief a time as I had logged

"THAT," he said, with a flourish
as he waved his Molson,
"Is Canadian Yew wood!"
& he said it as if it was pronounced from the Queen herself

The females have tiny red berries
but were no different in appearance
then the males, but that they were
dioeciously conifers with separate sexes
was something that seemed an oddity,
yews were generally few & far
between but in the right conditions
they would form stands that followed
the creeks downhill & appeared
as un-uniformed limby
gnarly red barked ever green twisted
with holes & grown
over defects that were as old as
the tall Douglas fir
their large European counter parts were used as chapels
by early Christians
who took them from
Pagan worshipers that found their otherworldly
appearance in deep forest as thin places
to be contingent with other worlds
& I who had formerly spent
my short forestry career in clearcuts
where all this had been raped,
well, the three weeks I spent with
Yews, kind of sealed this notion
They *were* other worldly,

So, yes, this separate place
was an amalgam
of earth, with a presence
all its own, we were surveying Yew
because its bark had been found
to be a cure for breast & ovarian cancer,
the worry at the time was
that we had cut too much of it
& the need for it for medicine would
be its demise in a few short years

notwithstanding the fact we had burned up
More than was left, calling it "trash wood"
perhaps every incurable disease has
its counterpart, in this manner
the European Yew were almost wiped out because
of its prize as a commodity for long bows,
As a millennium of war raged on that continent.

This is really more understandable
rather than the overuse because it was
"just in the way," of D-8 cats
& the ever present need to tidy up
& burn the left over's so we could entertain
The notion of growing back trees like corn that
had in a rather elegant fashion been growing to cure
the beloved's—the grandmother's,
the mothers, the young women whose
lives were to come into an age of
this life out of balance

Education formed for reductionist drones
so that in corporate discounting of the lovely,
& the obscure
into spreadsheets & bottom lines
while the checkerboard square clearcuts
of Pacific Northwest took away
the great bands of yew & the spotted
owl—who were never seen
as created harbingers of loveliness,
& health & the sure goodness of
hidden away answers
to all our problems

Two Eleven-Year-Old Girls Raped and Strangled

after the Cortez murders

Papers have headlined,
& the airwaves reported
events of last week...

Lord, this time
like many others You seem conspicuous
by your seeming absence

or is it always that
we are absent from
ourselves in such
vast numbers
you cannot make it
to all the sheep
before nightfall?
or did you know
the events before hand
in the vast immediacy
of this universe
of yours as it travels
the speed of light
experiencing no time,
leaving that & sorrow
to our own devices,
allowing dark evils
their own course?

I do not believe this is true,
were their Guardian Angels
napping? or taking
time out for a celestial dram?
or were they waylaid

by some other faraway pity?

or the next County?
do Angels make mistakes? & if not
how could they have watched? or,
very pointedly, who held them back?

I do not accept
an abstract drivel
about the all and everything,
in the natural course of events,
this instance being related
to cause and effect and destiny
or a hippy's notion of Karma

so, this is laid at Your feet
for an answer
& as these words are written
they do seem to wheel and come back,
& bite me & maybe
an answer

in the flippant
careless thoughts and words
absently let out
in an inattentive air
leaving gaps
in our guard
& good sense–allowing
evil its course, daily
or something on the other side to push it on us
because in this state,
You are selectively involved, &
every day, we forget to love...
every day.

These Pelicans

Four pelicans on a log downriver
Sit like squatting men
this crimson Sacramento River evening,

& one rises up a sleepy watchman
& slowly waves his wings,
As a good breeze blows upriver,

Paired mergansers begin to move away
As I sit down and look at the pelicans
Whose white through binoculars
become pink for a moment
With changing clouds & sunset
Coming

I've never wanted flamingos,
I've been waiting
For these damn pelicans to show,
& they sleep on the log

All the while I'm sitting under the cottonwood,
That release a snow-like namesake floating &
Blowing upriver, & mallards
Begin to sound and take air across the river

Two pair wheel & move upriver
Then turn again, chitter to each other
In flight & reverse & land
Near the shore below me
Across from the pelicans,

By me, the wild grape from
The cottonwood hangs dead
In the river having
Been broken from some flood,

The mallards wing away
Again, I catch them in flight
With my glasses,

These green heads
Winging with their brunette wives
Paired up noisily and across the river
I see the soil layers on the eroding
Riverbank that each lay down
On the valley long
Before the dam

There are two surfaces
Shimmering streaks with
After breaking water
Lines on the river
In front of me now,
& ten minutes ago,
There were three others, &
A ways down river
I see two more, &
As I walk to get oranges
From the neighborhood
Communal tree
I now know what the pelicans know.

The shad are in.

The House Was on The Corner

The house was on the corner
At the edge of a Kansas town,
Chinese elms in
Front yard & until I was seven
A large sycamore tree spread
Over the corner & diminished
The buzz of the grain elevators
Across the street but one day
The city came & cut it down
When my father was
Out of town, &
Even though it was my
Grandmother's tree,
She played under as a child,
As was I, that morning
& I remember her weeping
& wringing her apron
As it fell to the ground

The two-story home was built around 1900
West porch was slat board &
Screened in & had a little furniture, the front door
Was screened & then you came on the porch
& to a wooden door
With thumb button latch, & opaque glass
Gave way at waist height, walking through the
Door was a round oak dining room table of some size
A deer head mounted on the wall was from an era
Of lesser taxidermy skill
& was even a little ragged, as a child
But it was the only deer I'd ever seen
& my grandmother every Christmas
Put a red nose on this buck

There was a china cabinet about chest height
w/a narrow mirror
It was made of a dark stained wood
& in the bottom my grandmother
Kept my father's war medals,
a Silver Star & a Purple Heart
The ends of the cabinet that recessed
the mirror had posts
& one had a false front
That held papers unbeknownst to the casual eye
& a railroad watch, gold & jeweled
& inscribed to my grandfather

Beyond this room was the kitchen
& bathroom w/claw foot tub
Beyond that another screened in back porch
that also enclosed a trap door
To a cellar, for can goods,
& tornado warnings every spring & summer

& a dark cloud rumbled
& that certain prickly kind of feeling
hung in the air at night in May 1955,
& it all came up sudden
& the storm sirens went off &
& wind hit our house hard like a ship hits a rock
& I remember
Our dog being chained in the back yard
by the minnow tank
& from streetlights I could see him
Being stretched out on his chain by the wind,
& I'm grabbing for the door
To get him, as my father shoved me down
Cellar stairs, & the neighbors
in the little red house didn't come over like
They usually did
& the wind stretched the house frame

in an eerie creaking way
Then it all calmed down,
& we found out the tornado struck ground
In Udall sixteen miles north
& east of us, minutes later
& killed 87 people,
& the south half of that town was leveled,
& 200 were injured,
& my dog was alright & my grandmother
Stopped weeping for the Sycamore tree

Anger of a Kind

Anger of a kind
rests in the contours
of our palms,
inexpressible

Anger of a kind
with clenched fist
demands hearing of
why & wherefores
to this satiated life

Anger of a kind
bleeds from open wounds
& wombs, distended
bellies, machine-gunned children
nerve gassed children, & children
killed by suicide bombs

Anger of a kind
wretches at the politicos,
foreign & domestic,
whose wart-healing
short-term gain
infects itself & all
that it touches
with promises & putrescence's

Anger of a kind cries to a limpid
unconsciousness not
to accept anguish, suffering,
murder, ignorance, nor placation
solely because they have always been
or, because they have always been paid off

Anger of a kind stands
witness for all that come after,
sometimes
having used a tempered edge
for necessary deadly force
and final will for change,
& that swift bitch--change herself

This anger is kind

Death & Poetry

sometimes…
it comes hard
& cold like your
guts being blown
through your jacket
on a snowy afternoon
or soft, like…
a pile of barbiturates
& a bottle of whiskey
sometimes you can actually see it
in a cops breath,
or the newspapers,
or catch a glimpse of it
in the sidelong glance
after a lovers embrace,
sometimes it's a car wreck unexpected,
a skid & then the crash
& no good reason why you walked away
sometimes…
it is not there,
& then it is, as what it will replace
takes long walks through
concrete walls not knowing the
coldness of space,
as what you thought of as life,
was a yesterday of four forgotten
poems you wanted to write

Integral

sandpipers take formation
from the beach/tiny
wingflutter up
hundreds
a sight of motion wall
of movement
together separate integral
& connected aeronautical Mobius
form&contention
then away
to alight a distance
short of an incoming tide
visual concert
of communal fidelity
now,
individual
beach walking
sandflea eaters

Canticle for Duke

I thought of the news, El Salvador,
Nicaragua, Middle East, war
& rumors of war—thirty years ago,
a vast surge & constant since &
in this human sea all contained
in torrent & rage, as the abuse
or lack of human freedom rolls with
its urge in waves of unrest & anxiety

I thought of a friend's cousin Duke
who, thirty years ago last month
drowned in the Sea of Cortez,
I do remember the night before he'd spoken,
over dinner in a beach restaurant,
of how he had loved his children
who looked forward to him
coming home every night &
because they did —it was all worthwhile

He & his father-in-law at dawn
had picked an arm of the beach
where Mexicans never swam, because of
undertow & this current took them fast a half mile out,
& the older man was a better swimmer,
& tried to save him & could not &
Duke disappeared from the old man's grasp in a swell
& a Mexican on the beach gently
that first day said, *"Tres dias,"* then pointed
To the gravestones and rough crosses
Three hundred yards down the beach from where
We were standing, & I did not think of this as consequential

How we waited after futile search
in hired boats for three days to pass when then

his body did float in with gentle
lapping waves, changed as the sea
does change dead men, to come to
rest in front of this Mexican beach
cemetery, & how Ricardo had said the day
before in a dry tone, not void of sympathy,
"El Mar es mi amigo; pero el mar no pardona."

We are in this sea together, friends
in surge & struggle toward calm
we are not seemingly capable,
the command, "Peace! Be still!"
one which is far, yet near our own voice,
where waves of confusion
could be laid placid, while it is, we
unlike the sea, that must forgive,
& buoy up what can be the state
of confidence that we are alive &
in this life together, on earth as
in heaven, & the dead
taking what we cannot see to a slow
motion bottom of unconscious sway

This Abundant Life

I can no longer call them homeless, not because they are not,
I am not relegating them to the planet, nation, community,
or under an overpass, cardboard box, tent in blackberries
 & not because
I have seen families living in Africa
with as much—or much less...
I can no longer call them homeless
I chose to call them Rotarian
that we may work for relief of especial needs
of others out of good will
see plight, acknowledge pain, knowing
we all need four walls for this abundant life

I know a preacher who regularly sits among them
rarely preaching Jesus, because he often finds Him there,
but instead buys them cigarettes, gives clothes
& pocket-money for cheap wine,
brings them food, or a tent when he knows they would use it
all to relieve pain, prays with them when they ask,
directs them to missions & shelters if they do not know,
takes them to the emergency room if they need to go
Rotarian's in our midst, a few of them better than we,
when living a fast-paced life in conceit

Some of them are insane, some of them thieves,
all have had something stolen,
many without learned skill of hygiene this
left behind with four walls of normal life,

they wheel on, on bikes, grocery carts
in a whining dull roar of traffic,
all of our pain and bliss is somehow connected,
moments of delirious uplifting sunshine

& anguished biting cold, moving south,
a hitch-hike, &
hopping a protected end of a grain car
makes trek a possibility, peer-passed on
whispered knowledge
of the 'best missions' with good food &
where they will not shame you with their
'Christian message'

A past Christmas morning
I saw two

in back of my motel's
outside wall, under an eve, arms
& legs entwined for warmth,
but yet sparkling with frost,
asleep, on crisp north California
December asphalt

I know another preacher who gives them clean socks
washes their feet... if they will let him, he washes
them lovingly in warm water, & spreads
antibiotics over sores & soles
while he shares the Gospel...

I can no longer call them homeless,
these Rotarians who sometimes
righteously rage at being killed
& destroyed beneath this crushing wheel.

Del Santee's Irish Uncle

Del Santee's Irish Uncle
on his mother's side
was a hit man for the IRA
during the Easter rebellion & beyond
& had to leave for the states
around 1930, give or take
a couple of years,
his specialty having been informers,
& he'd whacked enough of
his traitorous countrymen that by
the time of his departure of
Irish soil it was quite
dangerous for his own
self to walk Dublin's city
streets in the daytime,
he had followed each assigned
Judas for weeks
until they would eventually
go to confession & then
he would shoot them on the front steps
of the church,
or, close to the front steps,
having given them a grand
chance at clearing their soul of misdeed
Del and his cousin, fifty years after all of this
took the old man to an Oakland A's
baseball game, as the former revolutionary
had grown fond of the American game,
& in the bottom of the ninth inning
of a close contest, the elder of the three,
excused himself from his younger charges
& quietly worked his way
into some rows of seats above them & tried
to kill a man, roughly his own age, with an umbrella.

Del said the old man claimed
"Sure, he was a traitor.." he had
missed because the man
had never gone to confession.

Del said, his Irish Uncle
went to confess
his own sins every day of his life
since he had left Ireland.

The Forester

He twisted his head
his blond hair and blue eyes
underneath the tin hat with
the rain dripping off the back, then
peered down at me and with a
shovel in his hand I got my answer:

"The clearcutting of Douglas Fir
in this particular coastal range is
better for the trees we plant,
better for the soil we plant them in,
better for the animals that live here..."
I shut him off for it was
a company answer, much like
a company recording
that repeats itself if you
have not anything better to do
but go on listening.

I finished planting a tree,
his answer did not bother me,
even when I raised up and saw
off to my left, a mud slide that had
been the side of a mountain and now,
was at the bottom of a ravine,
making good time to the Pacific.

The trees that had been there were
of no consequence either,
for as far as you can see
they had been all cut down.

I know a logger that would give
away his chain saw to be able to

confront a Sierra Club member
while standing on a stump in that exact spot,
and with a gleam in his eye he would say:
"Yep, that's the way to do a
logging operation. You cut 'em all down!
Look man! Now you can see!"

His answer meant full bellies
for three children and land payments,
the company man was answering for
people that shuffled lives and papers,
ate in fine restaurants whenever they want,
drove expensive German cars
and shipped whole logs to Asia.

I have learned to reconcile all of this,
it is the way things have been for a long time.

What I could not reconcile was that
later that same day I heard an elk bugle,
twenty minutes later a cable screamed
dragging a log uphill to a high lead show

and they were in the same key.

I saw Ted Barr Smiling

I saw Ted Barr smiling
That self-assured smile that Teddy smiled
Full of himself and his friends
I saw Ted Barr smiling down
a long shot freeze frame
off the railroad tracks from the back
of the Hersey street house
Where you could see halfway through
this little jumbled up town
I saw Ted Barr smiling at an empty
paint spattered easel
& the guitar stand, standing now on Union street
But I saw Ted Barr smiling from Clancy's Pub
In Dublin town and I saw Ted Barr smiling
in the Log Cabin on the Plaza & the "Good" Club
& I saw Ted Barr smiling at the oars in the small rowboat
through the morning mist
& the glass surface of Immigrant Lake
I saw Ted Barr smiling now a true new immigrant
on the shore we have yet to go.
It is where I saw Ted smiling on his friends
that loaded Teddy grin.
I saw that smile on Skidmore street
where a brush with death
Brought on an on rush of oil and sweat
& sweet fullness and life, lugubrious
Thighs and breast and haunch
& thigh and pert cheeked tongued
Women on canvass,
& I saw Ted Barr smiling on oil & death & long legged
Sex in our life's dance on pity and blood
& the half-light of the last of the last
Summer of a Century of so damn much pain
I saw Ted Barr smiling

Teddy who had never got caught
in the cobweb of what 'ought' to be
I saw Ted Barr smiling
at the piano keyboard on Union street
I saw Teddy smiling the blues,
I saw Ted smiling at us
I saw Ted Barr smiling at his one true piece of art
&his own Amanda
Proud father & he was
I saw Ted Barr smiling at us
that loaded fat Teddy grin
& I cannot pound these keys hard enough
to let you know his Howlin' Wolf growl
Because I saw Ted Barr smiling

After Last Call

the big dog greyhound
just left going south
& the cops picked up
an eighty-five year
old escapee from a rest
home, it is twelve o'clock
almost a full moon & the
wind whips waves some-
where in the north Atlantic
sea, there is three nickels
on this bar—all tails &
your smile this night is
worth a suntan in the Fiji Islands
or love after this
bar stool is one hour up
turned & the old janitor
sweeps the floor while
most of this town sleeps
and the greyhound whines
twenty-inch tires still
four hours from Frisco

Voyager has now left the solar system

red and blue strobe flashing
cruisers making way
for emergency or small sins
against the state
sedate homes fill windows w/light
& inner movement
as if the city & small towns & large ones
were urban box cars riding the slow surge
of the continents past a somewhere
in the midst of words being laid down
foundations–forming parameters
of love–by a ubiquitous universal knowing
that we are transceivers
for us, a long ago thought
for us to perceive ourselves amid background noise
in dark light years of emptiness
full of something & unending love
while it is, we are startled by new ancient wonders since,
volcanoes in Alaska, Washington, Pagan, Philippines
& then we saw several thousand on Io's fly-by
& while sliding past
Saturn's Rings we found
beauty of form reaching unsurpassed
& back again–miracles
like morning light on half-visible
breast w/long hair flowing over pillow
& spring smell with jasmine, or an unseen
moment before a flower fades
& Voyager has now left the solar system

All That Is Natural

Holding love
at arm's length
as hype gets
in the way
more, thought to be
better, rather
than there being
no such thing
as better but
only good
& part of what is...

Around the corner it is the same
evident individual difference
of selfishness
proffered like multiverse
of which there is no
evidence yet, when before
another is...
defined as breath

& even nonindigenous
European starlings can fly in unison,
a murmuration of starlings
& maligned as they are,
yet, they cranky nest & breed & feed
in small groups, then move off in
great black mobial swirls perceptive
& perceiving, an unseen morphic field
of each other proffering
them as one, moving
north or south on the continent
thought of as nuisance birds & could it be
that this other perceived nuisance of

all that is natural—will
perhaps one resurrected day, come home
to roost when we see information that
binds it all, with which
we perceive inception
beyond any physical realm
mystically becoming Supernatural?

Independence Day

The sufficient crowd
where the lean attitudes
      culminate
the town or the country
the outlying geography
of containment & submission
the giving in marriage
the man and woman of relation
the public parade of *Eros*
the missing meal of *Agape*
the barroom of *Philia*
It does seem Hollywood only likes adultery

The willful negation of *Logos*
      the tangible criteria,
as if the world were spun anthropically
      on fingertips
of our reason, the motion set
      the will cocked,
the remaining whimpering
      bang a mere
spot in space and time.

That a judgment by ourselves,
be primarily in ourselves
& may we have the grace
to be loving & kind

& in a weltering rush
& suck before dawn
A dream—the where of now
the here of it,
the breath of is, may this love
Bring us fruit, each & each of who
We are meant to be & have been all along.

Demoiselle

In the last part of that time of dusk
when shadows meet the first departure of light.
over three fingers of the river
a Great Blue Heron performed an aerial pirouette.

Down with wisped blue gray feathers braking air
and into one side of a small island,
a fan of tail, a wing dipping
and to the other side,
where eddies and small pools
held more frogs and minnows,
only to see a man fly casting and then
beat wings hard, around, and again upward
through reddened light–down river.

That moment, bare, infinite,
myself standing in sand,
exchanging cigarettes & amenities
with another fisherman,
whose back is turned upstream
to the sound of faster water
I could not call his attention to this sight
and continued our conversation, with the sound
of river as chorus–I remembered the long legs
of a woman I had met the night before, as
gray blue wings passed
slow and noiseless over our heads.

I planted in the Trinity Alps

Someday I will go to
the second growth forest
I planted in the Trinity alps
on Southern Pacific land on a ridge,
where every day at 4 p.m.
for three days
Navy jets roared over us
at treetop level shaking the
ground and our hippy asses, while
resting & drinking tall boys
after 7 hours of
bone breaking work, placing tiny
spruce in ripped soil w/ tiny roots
all landing in moisture &
packed down to spring out
next spring and grow back
to giant towers just before
the bare grassy alpine, if
& only if they are forgotten

First of Three encounters with Lions

I was about 15
Fishing on our creek
Then backed up by
A dam to irrigate, &
I was drowning worms
In a deep hole, the sky
Was dark from a forest fire
Near Prospect, & a guttural
Coughing noise came from the
Other side of the creek, my
Border collie, started to whine
& bark, become defensive,
I had no idea what was up
& she ran to the bank to where she
Could cross & once across she
Dove into the brush below an old high water
Cut bank topped with pine
& 40 feet from me, out came a cougar
Running like a cat, tail
Whipping for balance &
Bringing its hind legs in unison
Clawing earth & running away,
From my fierce border collie.

A Psalm

I have been excited by women
in libraries
followed movements with
my eyes as a sail fills
with wind and felt the jolt
like a prow taking
its cut through a wave

I have been excited by women
in libraries
whose slow surreptitious movements,
the turn of an ankle
short measured steps in high heels
a twist of mouth
a glance at a bookshelf
or through it

I have been excited by women
in libraries
whose silent voices echo chapters
of humility and respect
as peasant dresses
and pigtails flow by with ghosts
of Marilyn Monroe movie memories
and placid book cover art
I have been excited by women
in libraries
rolling book carts to proper shelves
cataloging history and
time and gossip and art

I have been excited by women
in libraries
crossing legs out of terry cloth dresses with

rouged cheeks and
red elevated lips
taking a book inward
with focus and cognition
while red hair
and white thighs exude
auras of creation

I have been excited by women
in libraries
as if Sappho's lost poems
appeared while I wait for
a tall dark-haired woman
to find me here between
stolid wooden shelves
where dreams meet the sea
and hearts have tried
to expose the sky

I have been excited by women
in libraries
and have turned pages
of desire toward islands of thought
where there are
rose petaled shores
of sure goodness
and love

St. Somebody's

Not that hospitals
Are not necessary if you
Need one,
I must admit
Other plans have
Not prevailed
But writing
This poem from
My phone in bed
Being better
Than the alternative,
& if this is the last
One, I would recommend the
One before
Though this
Is no dark
Thing I have been
Pulled back more than once, yet
A woman moans
From across the hall
From pain
While their pain protocol
Cannot help, she moans on & on
Most nurses do not want to bother Doctors
Some do & care
but the Clara Barton
Ministering Angels are not stopping for her, or
To inquire who is on the list, held back by
Triage & a corporate dice roll, an MD tells me
Hospital administrators lie to the sisters,
Despite the prayers of brothers,
Prayers of Fathers, prayers of Mothers.

Fall of the Hipeoisie (Hip-WA-ZEE)

She had been leaning
into him all six feet
of her Asian beauty,
her toes pointed out
red shoes below a tight green dress,
    as you drank your beer
you thought they were lovers
she was telling him whatever
& he is looking at his long hair
in the mirror
but she was adamant
in his ear as he blew smoke out his nose,
& looked at himself through sunglasses

he owned three hip record stores
around the valley financed largely by white powder..
& this was how he got his women
& then & then..
she,
body slammed him
off his bar stool!

she had him on his back
stood over him & screamed,
    "You motherfucker!"
At first everyone
Everyone thought it a joke
& then became quiet
& for a moment everyone stopped thinking
about themselves
as the juke box belted out a bass thud
reverberating thru the floor & then
falling with her knees on top of his chest
She hit him three times, a left,

then a right & another left & sd
"I AM a good person!"
& continued,
with a fist for every syllable,
"YOU-*are-a-moth-er fuck-er!*"

They pulled her off him,
three women &
a large Samoan man,

Then he got his skinny ass up laughing
& hesitated, & snarled
& then went for her, &
as she strained against the crowd,
    he wanted to hit her while the crowd held
    her back
    then he
got pushed back into the juke box
by another finger pointing woman.

Venus Void of course

Stepping out into
The crisp night air under leafless
Oaks, there is a clean
Smell that can only be
Had in certain places,
Venus shimmers off mountain
Horizon, I thought maybe
You were looking at her too

Glimmering off your Bodega Bay
The pliable ivory of your face & red hair
& connected pervasively,
Venus occluded with the moon
Four days ago.

While you know
I do not buy Astrology
& for you that's part
Of your faith & that is all right
For you then
I wonder about now

Three days before this evening
I am told of twelve people
Are meeting
Three of which believe
That they are from Venus
& have video tape of
Venusian spaceship
Landing on earth

Life is preciously beautiful
& we are part & parcel of
Gaseous formation of the adjacent
Planet & I would never want
To break up their meeting, & laughing
Though I am

Knowing that voiding time
All of this is a togethered thing &
While Botticelli's art
Which we accept unlike
The Venusian spaceship
& how he
Put her so delicately
Her on the half-shell
With your red hair

It is more like
A dream this art as life
Than a reverie
But there in imagination
We loved each other
& shared our last name w/out marriage
no relation & states away
A decade apart our
Birthdays, yet the same?

We astonished each other
You were swooped off
To California, but
In this cabin, this damn
Cold Oregon December,
Your red hair spilled across
My chest, your smell like
Lilac must, your
Touch soft, is soft &
Warm air becomes heavy
Acrid smoke fills the air,
A cabin, or a cave,
Or a peat heated shanty above
A wind-swept cliff & the sheep bells
Clang in the mist?

I saw a reflection in your eyes
Dim light, our bodies move,
& then we were still, & your
Touch again, it should not be
A dream, yet it was
& that is all we had

My heart surged
Not from desire
But from wonder &
Though we never made love, you
Were many times on
My arm & we many times kissed
Deep spit swapping passion
& one night we slept together
This imagination makes what it will
Yet you were always a person
Not to be worshiped
But to be known & we knew each
Other in some kind of morphic
Field that came together & said
Remember?

I do not buy reincarnation either, but
The neo-paganism you seemed to love, hey
The playful part I get,
Masks & drums & the anthropomorphic
Notion of animals, like coyote, but
The old gods have always been
Flipping dead
Pagan playfulness still has a black ribbon
Running through it to the diabolic,
As did the inquisition,
Or any religious spirit
In every camp—waiting
For the wrong move away
Presence interior & from
Above simultaneously

The dimness fades
& the light grows
Too, too bright
I close my eyes
Black ice & fire
On the moon
We were both void
of direction
Toward God

& then I see again your face
Surprised
Then calm, your face changes, again &
Ten out of ten of us die Kelly my love
& you were eventually gone

Why the Cold War was Cold

"It is," he said
After a long story
About how he worked
In missile silos,
For three
Years while
In the Air Force,
"the first time in history the
Ruling Class has had to worry
About starting a war."

Brief description of Creation

love made five animals
rising out of the sea,
the first, a colonial creature,
fastened to the rocks, ate what washed
by and showed itself on the lowering of the tide,
the second, wore a green cloak, ate of
the sun and covered the earth,
the third ate of the second and walked on the
earth indifferently, the fourth ate of the third
in an exclusive manner
the fifth ate of everything.

Mall Santa

The crowd looms
& I am a mild spectacle
Ho, Ho for dough
I smile, wave, & shout,
"Merry Christmas!"
At them all they want,
Yes, I believe &
Tell some of the nose miners
As I am led, that Christmas is *really*
About Baby Jesus, some of them know this
But I am forbidden to do this, by the hucksters from
New Jersey that run the photo business
The parents are generally having a good time
The Mall is reasonable, making
The concession folks let the parents take pics
On their phone camera, without buying, so all
Can sit on Santa's knee, buyers or not,
The poor are challenged by the $40-dollar snapshots
Insatiable consumerism?
Well, there are the little ones that
Really believe, the college students
Running the set are intelligent & need
The money, I am old and still
I think intelligent &
Need the money, though I cannot always
Remember all the names of the reindeer
I rattle off the ones I do know
& it always works
No one tests Santa,
Had I walked by this scene
& some other bearded fat man
was doing this, like in a Bruegel painting,
I would take no notice,
The line of children daily winds around,

Some of children want toys that total more than
One thousand dollars & some,
like the small smiling boy, from
A humble household by the look
of his smiling parents,
Asks only for "new slippers,"
& his thread bare brother asks for a "new coat"
& my heart wells up and the parents smile
& I know they will get them
& I say, "Why yes, of course you look
Like good boys to me,
Santa knows you are good boys!"
& I say the same to most of them & even
To the affluent, knowing if the thousands of
Dollars of tabulated excess does not all work out
Disappointment will help them as well,
& near Christmas after a lunch break,
I stride in the Mall with
A confident "HO, HO, HO"
& a little guy streaks away from his mother
& runs a hundred feet to me
As fast as his 18-inch legs will take him
& I sweep him up in my arms
& he holds tightly to my neck
& will not let go until his mother's arms are near
& the next day
This scene is repeated by another tyke
& now, I am 70,
& in this same manner
I long to run to the arms of God
& tightly hug His neck.

Starting just before 1970

The double standard was part
Of the unwritten rule
At the start of the decade of the seventies
rules were being bent,
made up, broken, thrown away
& generally laughed at.
It would not be until the mid-1980s
that the pandemic
of acquired immune deficiency syndrome
would bring us scurrying through the gutters
to find the rules and again adopt a modicum
of fidelity that had been temporarily
on hold while penicillin really had knocked
sexually transmitted disease easier to cure
than the common cold, oh these were the brave years
of a sexual revolution that was no more
revolutionary than tomato juice
Personal behavior as a consequence
was on hold with *Roe v. Wade* mixed up
privacy with infanticide, or reinstalled it
as a pagan rite, while My Lai could be rationalized & its
perpetrators could be slid into obscure exoneration
in the day it was Pendleton shirts,
& Converse tennis shoes,
V-8 engines that took you down the American highway
At a high rate of speed, the lonesome highways
between suburbs and rural America where you
could feel a rhythm of road noise
& drive in a day a distance
your grandfather could not travel in three weeks
& then there was the warm wet your pants
seduction of the commercial

national rant of it, that sold the notion
to the nation that this perfect thing
we thought we had, was never perfect, which it was not.
but the sales pitch was—that there was a sale
on Democracy worldwide & that, somehow made it right
that we had the right to make that illusion
part of everywhere else

a good number of people did not like this very much

Without God

Without God
We are inviable,
Despite prosperity
Or poverty,
As in a cockpit
Each auguring in existence
Has its play
On the subjective field
Here for the short term
Gone for the long
Invisible to each other's
Motives, deepened toward
Craved modality
Day to day
As categories
Each to the other unable really
To name oneself because of
That concern for self
As if we were used to be
Hobos crouching under
An overpass in any
Inner city's out skirted
Center
Boiling cauldrons of indifference
Missing a presence
& seeing only of past presents
& unabashed voiding of bowels
Under bridges of concept & conceit
As 10 ply tires whine on the pavement overhead

Tramp Harbor

We had fished most of the evening away
when I had hooked the bottom
of the sound
straining on the line
cranked the big spinning reel
at each giving of pull
strained on the line
forearms bringing up
something…
giving way a dead weight
lifted off the bottom with each
successive pull & no fighting
movement back
the line gave its monofilament whine
as I pulled straining upwards,
the letting go & pole dipping down
to reel in again,
then pull pole arcing upward a
weight of no live thing
coming to the top of the sound
rod bending hard and over
down and closer now
coming closer now,
the line with 2 blood knots now
tying three strands to
one, all bringing in
the end from the bottom,
comes closer now
the weighted form
from the bottom,
as from the dock we saw stretching
through water hand like, from
forward lighting only
from Des Moines across this Puget Sound

three miles of light flicker shown, to light
a form piercing air now
hand like with body following
in dim reflected light
we had joked about a body,
& now we were silent as up through a slack tide
came a small water drowned entire alder tree
with all its branches.
perhaps, that had fallen from
a cliff off Portage
& had rolled with the tide til then
& the "bite' was off
we packed our gear away,
stacked lifeless fish into a bucket
& left the darkness,
later my friend wrote a poem
about what it might have been,
it all stayed inside me a week
when it was, I knew why,
as it had been how they found my father

The Green Flash

She started a conversation
& then said, "There isn't any
More wine," then that finally
Ran down too,
With an economic ocean evening
& I looked, but it was not there
I had seen it before, & looked
Again, & some have not seen it
Some do not believe & others
Have never looked—but I have seen it
& it is there & sharing the similarity
Of being as sure as Jesus
& like Him it may appear when you
Are not looking, & it is said to be the
Phenomena of the tropics
& a bright by horizontal
Green flash that takes from a beach or boat
A good portion of the ocean horizon
Outward from the sun momentarily,
Then leaves as we twist round the corner
Into night & our own devices
& I have seen it in the Pacific &
In inhuman humidity where
Papayas ripen daily instead of in seasons
& there for some, just like Jesus again,
The knowledge of a cool northwest
Misty moss covered forest, or apples ripening
In the crisp fall, once-a-year— is unknown,
Except for the telling.

We are not human

We are not human
In the short run
As many tribes
Confine definition
Of humanity
To their own,
& we are not really
In our own as yet
Abstraction/loss
Being gain once seen
Looking upstream
The river pours toward us
So-called 'inanimate'
Belies presence
& then 2nd law of
Thermodynamics invents
Entropy, before survival
& now we know our stuff is from
Supernovas reaching back
& now forward
Looking downstream
The river pours away from us
Information is immaterial—that is really important
& together not natural as an explanation
We are this information & it is not natural
In & of itself because we perceive &
This clutching grip & explanation is
Supernatural, or Einstein was wrong
Now life, double helix'd in & life abundantly
But You, the Delivery vehicle?
Flipping off this universe
We are not human, save all of us
At birth or death or in between
Our humanity, our life is only human

Ghosts on file, until we know...
Because we are information
This place is not a one shot
Chance of pooling genes but
DNA defining an enigma & a Word
There was never any primordial soup,
Rather a spiral spoken Word...
Human only as we
Gently people
This earth seeing
Objective action we are
Containers of text &
Producers of text
3.7 billion year
lettered genetic message &
Each we are
Our names spoken
Together & ancestored
Up to now
History of time an inner
Missing of what is not, as
What is, that only human
Universal prosecution of background noise,
While either on fire, or on ice
We are made human by loving kindness
As a father runs to his children
Nothing can take this away
Blood having been shed &
A Word spoken before supernovas
As from that space dust we become this dust
To step into our home on the other side
Surprising all the stars because in the end
We are more important
Than the sun &
The Son is more important
Than everything

The Chink-oh-pin

It would be before
the gurgle of water
in streams clearing
after rains of after
stillness of the movement
of snowfall where
the chinquapin
& lodgepole take the first
winters weight of whiteness
all standing before moments
              pervasive & there
my heart leaps out for You
as a child kicking deep in
bellied womb, waiting as
the Cascades wait for each
winter's snow which is
cold slow birth of
every mountain spring

My Car

At eighteen I was driving my
Newly restored & shiny red 1951 Henry J
I had worked on for 3 years,
With its rebuilt, "Kaiser Supersonic 6"
Down Highway 62, it is 1967 & I hit
Black ice, swerved off to the right,
Over-corrected went into
A spin down the straight stretch of road
That sat atop a 10-foot roadbed being built
Over the valley floor, & was at that
moment frozen translucently
To the black top— late February, it's 11pm
I am coming back from my first real girlfriend's
Middle class tract home in Medford, Oregon,
but suddenly
I am spinning down the middle of the road &
As the little red car from the Highway
Is launched end, over end, through
The air towards a pasture I am thrown to the roof,
Then to the back seat, then back to the front seat, the
Next flip I'm in the back seat again, & the final spin
Rotates me again to the newly upholstered genuine
black Naugahyde front seats &
As it is coming down to the earth upside down &
Just before the crash landing,
The door opens & I am thrown out,
As the car top is crushed to the seats,
Sober, but young & not ever having asked for a miracle
Other than from my girlfriend I wanted to marry,
& knowing nothing of death, I pick myself up out of the mud
& with a minor cut on my leg, I screamed,
"My Car! My Car! My Car!"

Two voices from a campfire Long ago—or how, the dog Animal came to run w/man

"Let us go kill this dog
animal/use his fur &
eat of his meat

we can trap him
with snares
for he is greedy
for offal from the kill

his fur is thick
& sticks tight to
the pelt."

"No! He has keen
eyes of a hunter,
cares for his family
& is loyal to his mate,
he can smell the stag
two mountains away

Let us wait to
talk to him &
his wife, boast of
our kill, for this
year is very full

We will ask them
to run w/us, they
can smell out game,
eat their fill of gut
& then stay close

In the winter when the herds are gone,
then we can use their fur
& eat their tender children."

Hard Believing

This old man
he lay down on a couch
overnight invite to
sunrise, & service &
it had been three months
since he had read it,
& he lay down & he had not
prayed since a small boy,
& in his mind's voice he got out,
"Jesus,"
& an unearthly scream came out
his head & he
slept a sound sleep,
& woke refreshed
twenty days later having
listened to Father Louis &
how Dr. Williams actually preached
in *Paterson*, he
remembered, this night
& John's Gospel & then
reading, Psalm 22
he said yes, while the
'62 Chevy II
rolled across the bridge
on Antelope Creek, & he
canceled the Buddhist retreat & its
hard believing
39 years
& 24 rejecting
Church & state this old man
is gone

Wolves & Working Men
The Rape of Prince of Wales Island

Wolves took down deer working from
the beach & up drainages
In Southeast Alaska
They creep around huge spruce & cedars & ambush
Wintering deer in among windfall & beach driftwood,
With snow melt & deer moving inland wolves
Moved there into pockets of wintering,
Deer families in the central part of island
That never saw the ocean; the wolves took them there,
A vast sea of forest the size of Delaware
Which rippled over mountains & rose up,
From glacier made valleys, spruce, hemlock & cedar waving,
Slowly waving, as rain forest-
Rain soaked Foresters came hiking deep into the woods,
Up creeks & on out to ridges that stretched into the alpine
Laying out roads & designating units of "harvest' that
Laid out the boundaries of what would come next,

Wolves took down deer working from
The beach & up drainages
Loggers came soon & began to build roads
Craig & Klawok, then Hollis, Thorne Bay, Naukati,
Coffman Cove, & Hydaberg,
Cook shacks & bunk houses,
Began to appear, company stores sold snacks & cigarettes,
& Copenhagen cans of snooze,
each camp had a home guard,
Where a wife or two appeared,
State land came up for sale
Houses began to appear, rough at first then nicer,

Wolves took down deer working from
the beach & up drainages

Fishermen were already there mostly in Craig,
& native Klawok & Hydaburg,
But as houses sprang up,
There were more around the camps,
Bunkhouses, still housed men,
& float planes took them to "town"
meaning Ketchikan located on Revillagigedo Island,
The first city in southeast Alaska
Scores of bars & women & two days
If you could remember it was
Later called fun, no one thought it strange to send,
a float plane for pizza on Sunday

Men took down large trees, working from
The beach & up drainages
The pulp mills ate the Forest
Around Ketchikan, & began
To take down rafts of logs
From the Alexander Archipelago,
Alaska's storehouse, for the long straight grains
Of giant Sitka spruce that
Made everything from pianos & violins,
& in the 1800s were prized for ship spars
Then the pulp mill came and fiber slop
Was made & spun the forest towers
Into rayon for skirts, pant suits & blazers
& all the while then it replaced latex rubber
In the lower 48 with rayon strands woven in the tires as

Men took down large trees, working from
the beach & up drainages
Building roads & made their way to head waters &
Started working on the slopes,
The pulp mill ran three shifts, & the loggers came to town,
& still wolves took down deer working from the beach
& up drainages &
The roads began out of every logging camp

& gradually worked
Toward each other &
The central part of the island,
Each logging camp,
On the Island sea locked & remote, began to
Become villages with wives & children & schools,
 & little churches, & barged in groceries.

Men took down large trees, working from
the beach & up drainages
Around the Island & roads built of rock
& granite began to connect
& logging was money & jobs
Were plentiful & loggers tramped,
Their camp for another, with the same pay
Each time, a camp supervisor, or a Bull Buck
Did some stupid thing, too many mistakes,
Were made in the rigging, or food was bad
& with each bull shit thing there was more danger
& they began calling themselves
Tramps, with nose bag of thermos
& gear & duffle bags,
A sharp set of cork boots some of them
Worked the work, all over the Archipelago of Islands,
All making various stops,
Some of them set chokers some of them worked rigging
& some of them fell trees,
Some of them made it their life & some of them made
Money to go to college so they could,
Have a life; one timber faller,
Put himself through dentistry school
& bought cabin cruiser & he came back with his wife
To the islands every summer
For thirty years, long after the bunkhouses
& cook shacks were gone
Fixing folks teeth, & while tourists came
To catch halibut & salmon &

Men took down fewer large trees,
Working from the beach & up drainages

Big black bears always took salmon,
Working from the beach & up drainages
Splashing of spawning fish
Sockeye & pink salmon & dog salmon as well, while
The big black bear, the big belly draggers
Were noted in the outdoor press as largest
In the world & anyone could come take them
From all over the world
& the bear population that had outnumbered people
Came down without much notice,
& the locals seldom took bears for food
& generally, only in the Spring,
& the outdoor press became advertisements
& the lodges began
To sell package tours with a Suburban
& an Island map,
& with various expertise
Hunters came & bought tags,
& shot bears in the spawning streams
& drank liquor & wounded bears
& shot sows with cubs,
& drank liquor & shot bear,
& it did not take too many years
before everyone stopped seeing
Big black bear belly draggers
& the State sealers began sealing
Bear hides to the out of state hunter boys,
Teddy bear sized bears they had killed,
& sows were taken,
& the orphaned cubs, the poor orphaned cubs,
Showed up at the lodges meant for rich folks,
& even the ardent bear hunters
Began to call this wrong,
& the State in time changed the rules

After, a lot of the damage was done, on
Prince of Wales Island where nature
Was constant before 1954,
When the roads began to connect,
& the logs could go to the big mill in Craig
& little mills all over the island,
As the pulp mills were shutting down forty years later
When they & some of the foresters saw
A diminishing end of the thought
Of a never-ending supply

Men taking down large trees, working from the beach
& up drainages where now a patch work
Of timber patches made a mosaic from the air
No need to plant trees in the rain forest land,
Where the trees came back, but
The big trees were gone forever,
If the clearcuts were rotated
every 50-100 years, like well
Like, Aldo Leopold said, like cabbage patches

& like cabbage patch kids, boys & girls with degrees
Showing how this could all be managed &
Forest plans were planned,
& all the nations' laws were mentioned
& it was still that,
Men taking down large trees, working from the beach,
& up drainages
But they forgot about the wintering deer,
That became stranded in deep snow clearcuts
& politics were added to the industry of timber,
Some became fishermen, some lodge owners
& some started little mills,
& some roads became pavement over time &

Wolves took down deer working from
The beach & up drainages

& the villagers could trap, beaver, otter, marten
& wolves & kill deer for winter meat,
Salmon & halibut canned up was larder as well,
Protein was often immediate & had to be taken,
Like taking a coat along on a cold winter's day
Every household was allowed five deer per person
& a lot of Salmon
& halibut were canned up,
& frozen as well
& then in time some noticed not as many deer
& thought of the wolves & first blamed them,
While seeing winter range
Disappearing as big trees on trucks,
No one noticed for a while the dead fawns
That had nothing in winter to eat
They still saw boatloads of bucks
Coming in on Charter boats,

No one saw wolves killed on the beach just for fun,
Winters snow depth not letting the deer out of inland
Stands of refuge, & the Islands of refuge became,
Deer holding pens, this all came after time while still,

Men took down large trees, working from the beach
& up drainages

Slowly at first, tourists had arrived more every summer
& lodges appeared; charter boats caught too many
"Barn Door" Halibut named for their immensity
& pictures were taken & no one thought
Of these three hundred pound
Flat fish as the egg laying mothers,
That kept up the stock & behemoths were
Caught & butchered like bison on the plains,
& the pictures continued to be taken
& the stock started to slow,
The commercial fishermen were limited

to weeklong seasons
& tourists from Texas
& tourists from Tennessee,
Tourists form California, tourists from Oregon,
Tourists from New York, tourists from Minnesota
Came with thousands of dollars to spend &
Chicken Bay which was named for
The good eating "chicken halibut," flat fish
Of around twenty pounds, loggers in skiffs and tourists
Came for the chickens but
Their mothers were vacuumed away
& the big fish were all distant, at a several hour boat ride,

The summer brought traveler halibut from the far north,
& villagers long lined a year's catch enough every year
But the charter boats & everyone else
Took the big ones,
& the stocks began to wane,
& after arguing for some time, the biologists
Got a handle on this
& there were less charter boats & like the bears
Just in time, still...

Wolves took down deer working from
the beach & up drainages
Clearcuts in mosaic grew back plentiful forage,
Strings of mild winters
Let deer slip through wolves & men
& for a good time, deer numbers were up,
The roads adjacent to clearcuts
Were for a time shooting galleries each fall,
After hunting the alpine the deer lower down
Could be found in the clearcuts
& a high-powered rifle from the road
& nice buck would fall,
The rut would deliver more
& boats following the beach

Could come back with a boat load of bucks
To round out each families take,
Then charter folks began to do this

Men took down large trees,
No longer working up from the beach,
All the drainages were logged
leaving a bathtub ring of clearcut
Around all the Island's creeks
Save the centermost part & the Karta Wilderness,
& the Honker Divide
The inner portions of timber taken,
Were the deer winter range
& soon there was
Less & less of it, more roads, more hunters less deer,
& now there were less wolves to take down
Less deer working from the beach & up drainages
& men took to killing wolves, no longer working up
From the beach, but working up roads,
& no longer for pelts in the winter,
Men took to killing wolves, just
Because they were wolves
& they also ate deer, & the fewer wolves became few
Wolves in the central part of the Island

That, save the beach road on the Clarence Straight,
Was now surrounded by pavement,
& 4-wheel drive pickups could speed
From side to side of the island
& crawl up most roads until deep December
& hiking in & setting snares became
Predator control for the few that warred on wolves,
And called themselves the wolf patrol,

Some biologists called it the end
of the wolves upcoming,
& others said they would be alright,

But when they started to investigate
the wolves were down to a few,
& the few became three & the dens
were all empty save one,
& it would be some time
even then if measures were taken,

Wolves once again took down deer
Working from the beach
& up drainages
& if the central island wolves disappear.
there are still packs to the north though not very many,
& packs to the south, though not very many,
& maybe they will come back
Just like the halibut and bear the biologists disagreed,
& some say the winter range can be logged
& others say it cannot, three or four wolves taking,
down deer working from the beach,
& up drainages
& now there are court cases and the
Small numbers of wolves are apparently inbreeding,
& lawyers & judges to decide whether
Wolves will still take down deer working from
Beach & up drainages.
& for a time, the government wanted to suspend all the laws
To send the logs to China
Instead of the mills on the Island
& no one knows how long wolves will still take down deer
Working from the beach & up drainages
Long or short term
      —this tragedy of the commons

Sunflower heads

I put two large
Sunflower heads
On the railing of
My deck overlooking
The river a month ago
& a titmouse
Is taking a meal now,
When I had commercial
Bird seed there, every bird
Seemed to come around,
Now there are only four,
I should say Titmice,
Because, well it is fun to write Titmice
As I look over my coffee
& this small action, a
Blue heron flies upriver
& his grey blue slow beating wings
pass the early light & flashed a
Bright blue through the tree forks
As sunlight hit the wispy feathers, &
Just to the right toward my neighbors well-kept yard,
Two snowy egrets pass downriver &
Three hummingbirds fight
At their feeder, on my deck while NPR
Tells me there are war planes
Once again to Iraq,
As some Muslims are beheading
Journalists and children &
Crucifying Christians in open squares

Love is like

Love is like a changing
flight of small birds
through a snow flurry,
that though it is,
they have never paid
the rent two days late,
or had a shut off notice
for a late electric bill
appear on the front door,
yet it is--they know of unseen seeds
amid whiteness and moisture,
there but to be looked for,
unworried in the finding
and its integrity,
as confusion becomes
what the wind whips
and not the wind itself,
so much is taken care of
in the on rush of life,
making doubt and insecurity
a snowflake
dissolving beautifully
on your arm.

First Contact

complex
the scion of ourselves
together,
Jesus coming in a leather jacket,
love being binding truth
whatall & why not w everything
connected to everything else
the small joke being incessantly
onus, the sleepers, compartmentalists,
bureaucrats, casual Buddhists, fundamentalists,
clients, zombiebodies in the unemployment line,
the men's business breakfast, all up
& down cannery row
save the faithful @ mass
but all equally guiltily asleep
in the church, the chapel, the synagogue, the mosque,
the buddha boy's temple
& everywhere else & the numbers
click & tabulate & go 'round,
as the gas pump goes 'round
there's been a lot of hands reaching up
there's been only one reaching down
& the all in all being
accounted for in an extraterrestrial plexus
of where we've been
where we're going
& what we shall be ...or
or cease to be
unless there is—First Contact

At the Counsel of Oak Flat

On the right bank of the Illinois River three miles above its mouth 22nd of May 1856, Chief John said to Lieutenant-Colonel Bnehanan:

"You are a great chief.
So am I, a great chief.
This is my country.
I was in it when these trees
were very little,
not higher than my head.
My heart is sick fighting the whites,
but I want to live in my country.
I will not go out of my country.
I will, if the whites are willing,
go back to the Deer Creek country
and live as I used to do among whites.
They can visit my camp and I will visit theirs.
But I will not lay down my arms
and go to the reserve.
I will fight.
Goodbye."

Chief John then walked into the forest.[i]

Tecumtum ("Elk Killer"), also known as Chief John, was chief of the Etch-ka-taw-wah, a band of Indians who lived along the Applegate River in southwestern Oregon.

[i] History of Southern Oregon, 1884 A.G. Walling p.279

Bear kill on deer hunt

Talk softly to the Bear
in his dying, apologize
profusely—commend him
his courage as he stood
before you—stood! mind you
stood upright as you
before his death,
your own self,
you who pulled the trigger
and sent the bullet
meant for venison
that ripped out his throat,
five yards from your own.

Talk softly to the Bear
in his dying, apologize
remorsefully, commend him
his life as connected
to your own
& from your perspective
in a lasting way,
for he would have killed you
or left many scars.

Talk softly to the Bear
in his dying, apologize
with wry humor
make a fine rug of his brown hide,
commend him his courage of life & spirit,
every time you walk by
but disparage his intellect,
tell him he should have kept
running from your partner
who stumbled through

the manzanita brush patch
that was his hiding place
with an unloaded gun.

Talk softly to the Bear
in his dying, apologize
sincerely, commend him
his spirit–send it back
to where it came,
as he lays next to
the knic-ki-knick leaves,
know the sound he makes...
"UHHNNNUUUUUU!"
Remember this all your life.

Living the Dream

I entered a fast-food restaurant,
My brand, where they will serve
Breakfast 24-7 & where I've never
Been sick afterwards, & this knowledge
Is valuable much like entering
An area in remote Indonesia & figuring out the
Friendly tribes & how to avoid the cannibals,
I & my wife walk up to the counter,
An affable Chicano dude
Takes my order, while giving others in the
Kitchen orders & I ask him how he is doing?
"Living the dream!" he says,
"Living the dream," he repeats,
"And you sir?" he asks.
"Wonderful!" I reply, "Wonderful!" I repeat.

Now I've been sitting in my backyard,
Remembering this & taking in my
Flowering light lavender purple crepe myrtle,
With finches eating
Thistle seed from the hanging socks,
My wife has tied there,
In this twenty-foot tree the finches are hanging
Upside down on the sock, like yellow monkeys &
Loud red and orange Canna Lilies
in the corner of the yard & now bright
New Red Crepe myrtle, is coming in
Beside the compost box, at breast height
Flowering for the first time deep purple red,
I am making small talk with my wife in this noise &
We are on a back deck under an umbrella,
At 10 am drinking good coffee
& it will be 104 degrees today, but now it is so pleasant &
I am remembering this breakfast two weeks ago &

Thinking about "living the dream," this gentleman
Had lots of tattoos, and deep scars on his face
& forearms—clearly some of his dreams had been
Nightmares, & there was a tone of
Sarcasm in his reply, & so much of this life
has been this ever-rewarding notion that
I am living the dream, while the poems
& stories come out & scream out sometimes
or sometimes softly, but I am finally living the dream
& the small pension and social security
are like the Guggenheim,
I never applied for, nor even wanted to apply for,
& this notion of the artists' life having to have
the day job, & wait, & while
I did both, I waited, did the bidding of others
for decades & some of it hard labor
& now I get to fish when I want
drive this word processer all day
Or fifteen minutes if I want
& I am taking all this in and paying
Attention dutifully to what my wife is saying,
& then she leaves & more
Finches come, a beautiful small red
& blue grosbeak comes to the
Bird feeder & peeks around the foliage,
leaves, comes back leaves again,
& comes back and feeds, I notice robins
in the grape vines on the white picket
Fence & realize they are eating,
our grapes that have just ripened, I yell
At them, & my wife has come to find out
What is going on & I tell her about
The grapes & we both go to inspect, &
Well, they have hammered all fifty or
sixty bunches of table grapes
That we were waiting to pick tomorrow, &
my wife is mad & I'm out on the other side

of the fence laughing at the birds & they picked
Clumps clean that were just here yesterday
pumping up their white green
Sugary goodness & are now skeletons
beneath the yellowing leaves, & yes
I am living the dream—I too have scars to prove it,
I have escaped death
More than once & like the sweet gone grapes
It is particularly good this given life
& its mortal expanse & well even
Last year the neighbors picked the grapes
while we were on holiday…

And the Fires We Talked About

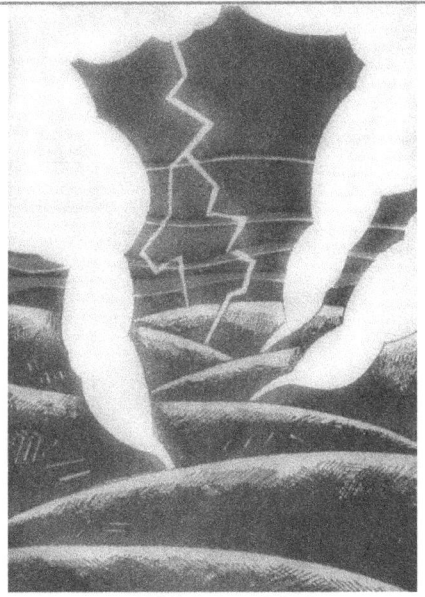

Stories
by James Ross Kelly

For this and more books by UnCollected Press:
www.therawartreview.com

www.ingramcontent.com/pod-product-compliance
Lightning Source LLC
Chambersburg PA
CBHW020942090426
42736CB00010B/1230